TECH TROUBLESHOOTERS

CONNECTING A COMPUTER SYSTEM

LISA IDZIKOWSKI

PowerKiDS press.

New York

Published in 2019 by The Rosen Publishing Group, Inc.
29 East 21st Street, New York, NY 10010

First Edition

Editor: Elizabeth Krajnik
Book Design: Reann Nye

Photo Credits: Cover vgajic/E+/Getty Images; pp. 5, 19 Hero Images/Getty Images; p. 6 oneinchpunch/Shutterstock.com; pp. 7, 11, 17 wavebreakmedia/Shutterstock.com; p. 9 michaeljung/Shutterstock.com; p. 12 panuwat phimpha/Shutterstock.com; p. 13 Casezy idea/Shutterstock.com; p. 15 Straight 8 Photography/Shutterstock.com; p. 16 Rawpixel.com/Shutterstock.com; p. 18 GaudiLab/Shutterstock.com; p. 21 T.T./Iconica/Getty Images; p. 22 KT images/The Image Bank/Getty Images.

Cataloging-in-Publication Data

Names: Idzikowski, Lisa.
Title: Connecting a computer system / Lisa Idzikowski.
Description: New York : PowerKids Press, 2019. | Series: Tech troubleshooters | Includes glossary and index.
Identifiers: LCCN ISBN 9781538329573 (pbk.) | ISBN 9781538329559 (library bound) | ISBN 9781538329580 (6 pack)
Subjects: LCSH: Computer networks–Juvenile literature. | Wireless Internet–Juvenile literature. | Computers–Juvenile literature.
Classification: LCC TK5105.14 I36 2019 | DDC 004.6–dc23

Manufactured in the United States of America

CPSIA Compliance Information: Batch #CWPK19: For Further Information contact Rosen Publishing, New York, New York at 1-800-237-9932

CONTENTS

A COMPUTER SYSTEM NETWORK

Life without computers is hard to imagine. Whether you're playing a favorite game, sending a birthday wish to your grandma, or staying in touch with friends, computers make everyday tasks easier!

There are many types of computers. Desktop personal computers—or PCs— laptops, notebooks, smartphones, and tablets all help people do their jobs and stay connected. Interestingly, computers can work in two ways—on their own, or as part of a network. A computer network is a group of computers and other **devices**, such as printers and scanners, that are connected to each other.

Tech Secrets Decoded

Don't give up on handwriting just yet. Studies show that children who write by hand learn how to read faster, store knowledge longer, and are more creative.

In school, students often work on computers that are part of a network. They can share data with each other, teachers, and anyone else who's on one of the network's computers.

5

WHY HAVE A NETWORK?

From the early 1940s until the mid-1970s, computers were very large and expensive. Later, computers became affordable enough for personal use. Today, it's common for a household in the United States to have several computing devices, such as a desktop computer and smartphones for each family member.

Tech Secrets Decoded

A 2016 study shows that 51 percent of young adults between the ages of 18 and 29 years old in the United States live in a household that has three or more smartphones.

Families often use their computing devices when they're together. One person might be sending emails from their smartphone. Another person might be surfing the Internet. Someone else might be streaming a movie on his or her tablet. Being connected to a home network can make all these activities possible.

NOT JUST AT HOME

Computer networks aren't used just in people's homes. Many places in your community depend on computer networks. Schools, libraries, hospitals, police stations, grocery stores, banks, restaurants, and other businesses need computer networks to do work and keep people connected.

Small towns, large cities, and even entire countries count on computer networks to do work every day. Trusted networks provide people with many different services. Imagine how many networked computers are needed to keep a busy airport on schedule and the planes flying safely. Networked computers in grocery stores keep track of what foods people buy the most so that the store doesn't run out of them.

Tech Secrets Decoded

The U.S. government created the first computer network, known as the Arpanet. One computer was in a lab at UCLA and the other was at Stanford—350 miles (563 km) away.

Doctors, nurses, and other health-care workers can share information about a **patient** using networked computing devices.

9

HARDWARE

The **hardware** in a home network might include a number of computers and smartphones, and maybe even a printer, a scanner, or an e-reader. Large networks, such as those in a large office building, connect these same types of hardware, but there are usually more of them.

Large networks—and some people's home networks—have a **server**. Many schools use servers. Each computer or computing device in the school may be connected to the server through the network. When a computer requests, or asks for, something, such as a file, the server finds and sends that file to the computer that requested it.

Tech Secrets Decoded

Network computers follow protocols, which are certain sets of rules and instructions computers use to talk to each other. Protocols help the connected hardware operate correctly.

When a server isn't working well, computer **technicians** are called in to fix the problem.

11

WIRED OR WIRELESS?

Computers can connect to a network in two ways. A wired system has wires or cables attaching the networked computers and devices to each other. Early on, all computer systems were connected this way.

Tech Secrets Decoded

Many public places have areas called hot spots where wireless devices can connect to the Internet.

Without wireless routers, many people couldn't connect their computer to a network or **access** the Internet.

Today, most hardware devices, such as laptops and printers, are wireless, which means these devices can connect to form a network without wires. Wireless networks use a **router**, which sends radio waves through the air, allowing computers and other hardware to connect to each other and the Internet.

Laptops, tablets, smartphones, printers, and other smart devices use wireless networking **technology**. As long as there's a connection, this technology can work whether you're at home, school, or even at the local skatepark!

THREE NETWORKS

There are three main types of computer system networks. A LAN, or local area network, is the smallest of these three. This kind of network is used in schools, businesses, colleges, and other places where the computing devices are close together or in nearby buildings.

A MAN, or metropolitan area network, is a larger type of network system. These networks connect larger numbers of computers and groups of computers located in different buildings. This type of network can connect entire cities.

A WAN, or wide area network, can connect billions of computing devices. The Internet connects multiple WANs.

Tech Secrets Decoded

As of 2017, about 3.6 billion people around the world were using the Internet. That's nearly half the world's population!

The Internet allows people from all over the world to share information, or knowledge and facts about something, and talk to each other.

15

WHAT ABOUT SECURITY?

When you leave home, do you always lock the doors? When you ride your bike to school or the store, do you lock the bike up before you go inside? It's just as important to practice safety with computing devices as it is to practice safety with your home or personal belongings.

Tech Secrets Decoded

Many computers have built-in security software. A **firewall** works to protect computers connected to a network or the Internet.

It's fun to spend time on the computer with your friends. Just remember to keep your passwords to yourself and remember a few safety tips.

Creating a strong password is a good way to keep your information safe. Be careful which sites you give access to your personal information, such as your birthday or address. Don't open email files or **attachments** from people you don't know. Make sure your computers have up-to-date security **software**.

A CAREER IN SYSTEM DESIGN

Do you like computers and technology? What about solving problems? A career as a computer network **architect** might be a good job for you when you're older. The work of a computer network architect can be interesting and challenging. They work in offices and labs and with people and computer hardware and software.

Tech Secrets Decoded

Computer network architects will be needed in the years to come. The number of workers required for this career is expected to grow.

It's never too early to start thinking about what you'd like to do when you're an adult. If you like computers, work with them as much as you can right now so that you're prepared for the years to come.

Are science and math some of your favorite subjects in school? Computer network architects study computer science, math, and English in high school. After that, they study computer science in college.

Someday, you might find yourself planning computer networks for schools, businesses, banks, or even the local police station!

THE INTERNET

By 1976, there were 63 computers connected to the Arpanet. People created other networks, too, but these networks couldn't be joined.

The modern-day form of the Internet wasn't invented until the 1990s. The Internet is a network of networks, and it has forever changed the way people do what they do every day.

Today, many things, such as computers and smartwatches, can be connected to the Internet. However, as time goes on, people may be able to connect even more kinds of devices. The **Internet of things** is changing the way people live.

Tech Secrets Decoded

The Internet of things could change how doctors care for their patients. Patients with certain illnesses could wear a device that tracks their health, allowing doctors to find out when a patient needs treatment.

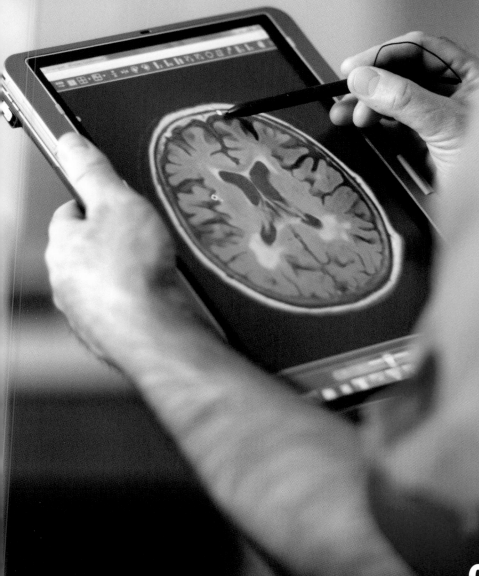

Over the years, advances in technology have changed the health-care field. The Internet of things is just one of these advances.

HOW ABOUT THE FUTURE?

No one knows what the future may hold. When your grandparents were young, they likely didn't think it would be possible for people to have personal computers, let alone have computers that fit comfortably on a desk or in the palm of their hand.

One thing is for certain. Computer scientists will continue asking questions, doing experiments, and solving problems. Because of this, more computer networks and connected devices will fill our lives. In the years to come, we may have even more smart devices to use and connect to networks!

GLOSSARY

access: The ability to use or enter something.

architect: A person who designs and builds something, such as a building or a computer network.

attachment: A file sent in an email.

device: A tool used for a certain purpose.

firewall: A computer program that keeps people from using or connecting to a computer or a computer network without permission.

hardware: The physical parts of a computer system, such as wires, hard drives, keyboards, and monitors.

Internet of things: The network of household devices and other items that can send and receive data through the Internet.

patient: A person who receives medical care or treatment.

router: A device that makes it possible for computers to send and receive packets of information to each other and over the Internet.

server: The main computer in a network, or group of connected computers, which provides files and services that are used by the other computers.

software: The programs that run on a computer and perform certain functions.

technician: A person whose job relates to the practical use of machines or science in industry, medicine, or another field.

technology: A method that uses science to solve problems and the tools used to solve those problems.

INDEX

WEBSITES

Due to the changing nature of Internet links, PowerKids Press has developed an online list of websites related to the subject of this book. This site is updated regularly. Please use this link to access the list: www.powerkidslinks.com/techt/connect